SPARK

by Andrea Debbink ✦ illustrated by Emily Balsley

Editorial Development: Darcie Johnston
Art Direction and Design: Dan Nordskog
Illustrations: Emily Balsley
Production: Jeannette Bailey, Caryl Boyer, Kristi Lively, Cynthia Stiles

Dear Reader,

Are you bursting with so many dreams, inventions, and ideas that you don't know where to start? Does an empty page inspire you or frustrate you? Do love to perform, invent new recipes, or compete in robotics? Or are you still figuring out what you like and how to express yourself?

Maybe everyone tells you that you're creative.

Maybe no one does.

No matter who you are—or what other people say—this book is for you. Everyone has the ability to create. You just need to give your creativity a chance.

It might help to have a guidebook—something that will take you along the path from having an idea to turning it into something you can hear or see or touch. This book is your guide. It will help you dream up brilliant ideas and turn them into brilliant things. You'll have some "just okay" ideas, too, and even some "not-very-good-but-interesting-anyway" ideas. It's all part of the creative journey.

This book will also help answer questions such as "What can I draw?" "What can I write?" and "What can I invent?" Along the way, you'll learn about yourself and discover new ways to let your creativity shine.

There's one thing to remember as you read this book—make it yours. Write in it. Take the quizzes. Fill in the blanks. Do the activities. Your handwriting doesn't have to be perfect. Your ideas don't have to be amazing. There are no wrong answers. We hope this book sparks your creativity. Here's to a brighter you and a brighter world!

Your friends at American Girl

CONTENTS

IMAGINATION IS THE ONLY KEY to the FUTURE. WITHOUT IT, NONE EXISTS. WITH IT, ALL THINGS are POSSIBLE.

—Ida Tarbell
Journalist & Teacher

CHAPTER ONE:
CREATIVITY

What is creativity?

You might think that **CREATIVE = ARTISTIC.**

This definition is a good start, but being creative is not the same as being artistic. Being artistic is only *one way* to be creative. You can dislike drawing or pass on painting and still be creative.

You also might think that creativity is a talent that some people have and some people don't. Maybe you've noticed your classmates labeling one another. Aisha does well in art class so she's the creative one. Sadie is on a swim team so she's the athlete.

But creativity isn't a talent that's possessed by a few lucky people or a skill that applies only to a few specific hobbies.

Creativity is the ability to use your imagination to:

- Come up with new ideas
- Solve a problem
- Add beauty to the world

- Communicate something to others
- Express who you are
- Entertain

In other words, creativity is an ability that everyone has and a skill that everyone can learn to use. A more helpful way to think about creativity is

CREAtive = HUMAN

or even better,

CREAtive = YOU.

CHOOSE YOUR CREATIVE INSTRUMENT

Because creativity is a skill, it looks different from person to person. Some people express their creativity through music or cooking. Others may use it for developing video games or choreographing a gymnastics routine or studying the stars.

Think of a school band. Everyone plays an instrument, but not everyone plays the same instrument, right? A band of flutes would sound okay, but it's much more interesting when you add drums, a couple of tubas, some trumpets, and maybe a glockenspiel.

Like a band that sounds better with many different instruments, the world is a more interesting and exciting place when people use their creativity in unique ways.

Still wondering whether you're creative? Sometimes being creative is simply a matter of finding your "instrument"—your favorite **way** to use your creativity.

Or your favorite **WAYS**.

HALL OF CREATIVITY

When you think of creative people, you might think of current celebrities such as your favorite actors or musicians. But many people throughout history—and today—have used their creativity in meaningful ways. Here are some of them. You may know them. You may not. Either way, maybe their stories or creations will inspire *you*!

COSTUME DESIGNER

ASTRONAUT

CHEF

SCIENTIFIC ILLUSTRATOR

ASTRONOMER

ARTIST

MUSICIAN

PHOTOJOURNALIST

ARTIST

ATHLETE

INVENTOR

ARCHITECT

11

DR. MAE JEMISON
Astronaut

As a young girl in Chicago, Mae Jemison dreamed of being a dancer, but she also loved science and wanted to explore space. In 1992, Jemison's dreams came true when she became the first African American woman to travel to space. Throughout her astronaut and medical career, she still found time to dance and do choreography. She even built a dance studio in her house!

ALICE WATERS
Chef

Alice Waters grew up eating vegetables grown in her backyard, but she really fell in love with fresh ingredients (and cooking!) when she studied in Paris. Her books and award-winning restaurant have taught a lot of people about food—from starting gardens in their own communities to turning fresh produce into delicious meals.

MARGARET E. KNIGHT
Inventor

Margaret Knight always had a knack for machines and mechanical things. She developed her first invention when she was 12! She eventually earned so many patents (27 in all) that she was compared to Thomas Edison. Her most famous invention is a machine that makes flat-bottomed paper bags, the same grocery bags we still use today.

DOROTHEA LANGE
Photojournalist

A childhood illness left Dorothea Lange with a physical disability that made it difficult to walk, but she used that challenge to become a documentary photographer. Despite the heavy camera equipment and slow transportation of the early 20th century, Lange traveled the United States and the world telling stories with photos. Her photos of ordinary people helped others understand important events such as the Great Depression and World War Two.

EDITH HEAD
Costume Designer

When Edith Head was first hired by a Hollywood movie studio in 1923, she didn't have any design or drawing experience. In fact, she once said the only thing she could draw back then was the ocean! But she worked hard and took extra art classes. By the end of her career, Head had designed costumes for more than 400 movies and TV shows and won eight Academy Awards for her work.

MAYA LIN
Artist

Maya Lin is an artist and designer who's best known for her public art and sculpture. She was just 21 years old when she entered—and won— a design competition to create the now-famous Vietnam Veterans Memorial in Washington, D.C. Today her large-scale art can be seen at parks, universities, libraries, and historical sites.

ELLA FitzGeRALD
Musician

Legendary singer Ella Fitzgerald was naturally shy, but her shyness melted away as soon as she started singing onstage. In the 1940s, her original style and vocal range earned her the nicknames "The First Lady of Song" and "Queen of Jazz." Using a technique called "scat singing," she could imitate nearly every instrument in an orchestra. In 1967, she was the first woman to be honored with a Grammy Lifetime Achievement Award.

IBtiHAJ MUHAMMAD
Athlete

Ibtihaj Muhammad is a world-class fencing champion—and fashion entrepreneur—who was the first American Muslim woman to win an Olympic medal. Muhammad was competitive from a young age and discovered fencing when she was 13. Today, in addition to being an athlete and sports ambassador, she manages her own clothing line with her sisters.

MARY BLAiR
Artist

Mary Blair was an artist who worked for Walt Disney's animation studios starting in the 1940s. After graduating from art school, Blair began her career as a sketch artist and watercolor painter. Blair's vibrant, modern illustrations influenced many well-known characters, movies, theme park attractions, and future illustrators.

WANG ZHENYI
Astronomer

Wang Zhenyi was an astronomer, poet, and mathematician who lived in 18th-century China. In a time when most girls didn't go to school, Zhenyi taught herself astronomy and mathematics using her grandfather's books. She made many scientific contributions, including conducting a famous experiment in which she demonstrated how solar and lunar eclipses work.

KAREN BRAITMAYER
Architect

Karen Braitmayer wasn't always interested in design. But after college, she discovered that architecture gave her a way to be creative. Today Braitmayer applies her skills, imagination, and experience using a wheelchair to design buildings that everyone can use. In 2014, she was appointed by President Obama to serve on a government agency that helps make buildings more accessible.

MARIA SIBYLLA MERIAN
Scientific Illustrator

Maria Sibylla Merian lived in the 17th century, when most people were afraid of insects and didn't think women should be interested in science. Combining her love of art, science, and the outdoors, Merian painted hundreds of detailed insect illustrations during her lifetime. Along the way, she made important scientific discoveries about the life cycles of plants and butterflies and other insects.

15

IN HER WORDS

Listen to this advice from even more real-life women
who use their creativity every day!

CHRISTINE LLEWELLYN
Pattern Designer/Artist

I figured out my favorite form
of creative expression by being open
to trying as many new things
as I could.

VERA BROSGOL
Artist/Illustrator/Author

There are so many different ways
to tell stories. I've tried comics, prose,
animated films, and picture books. My
job has changed but that has always
been at the core of what I do—
storytelling can be a part of your
life no matter what
form it takes!

As hard as it is
(especially given the presence
of social media), try your best not to
compare yourself to others. It will
always seem like others are doing more,
producing more, and achieving more
than you. Create and share as much as
possible. Compete with only yourself
and learn as much as possible
from your mistakes.

KIM WOOZY
Action Sports Athlete/Filmmaker

I love to skateboard and snowboard. I feel the most creative when I'm on a board. To me, choosing where I'm going to go, which turns to take, and what tricks to do feels like drawing on a blank piece of paper.

Everyone is creative! There is no such thing as someone 'not being creative.' If you feel that you are not a creative person, it just means that you haven't tried enough yet. My advice is to give up being scared, thinking you aren't good enough, or trying to get it right and just go for it!

LISA GRAFF
Author

Being a creative person doesn't always mean dreaming up great stories or painting beautiful pictures. Every problem in your life is a chance to be creative—whether you're trying to make cupcakes for a friend with allergies or fit all your socks in a tiny dresser drawer. Sometimes it's in navigating the biggest roadblocks that we end up finding the most interesting sorts of places.

CREATIVITY CHECKLIST

Now that you've discovered some ways other people use their creativity, what about you? Draw a heart around each activity you do, and draw a circle around each one you'd like to try.

WRITE STORIES

DO WOODWORKING

PLAY SPORTS

 GROW PLANTS

CONDUCT SCIENCE EXPERIMENTS

DECORATE

CREATE STOP-MOTION

COOK or BAKE

Act

SEW

SOLVE ? MYSTERIES

CODE

CHOREOGRAPH DANCES or ROUTINES

DRAW

BUILD ROBOTS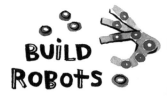

PLAY an INSTRUMENT

READ

SOLVE EQUATIONS

INVENT GAMES

DESIGN CLOTHES

EXPLORE NATURE

DRAW COMICS

DANCE

STYLE HAIR

SCULPT WITH CLAY

DAYDREAM

SOLVE PROBLEMS

PAINT

CREATE OUTFITS

 TAKE PHOTOS

SING

BUILD TOY SETS

CREATE VIDEOS

DO CRAFTS

Yes

No

NOTES

Having fun with my friends

What's your favorite part of creating?

The process

I like always having a project to do.

The sense of accomplishment when I'm finished.

Why do you want to create something?

Yes

I'm bored!

CURIOUS & COLLABORATIVE

You have inspiration to spare and time to let your imagination roam! If you don't have friends over already, invite a friend or sibling to join your creative adventure and bring supplies to share. Together you can create a video, build a model city, cook a meal, or go on a photo safari in your backyard.

SLOW & STEADY

When it comes to creating, you're not in a rush to the finish line. You might like a project that lets you work in small bursts of energy over time. Depending on the activity, you can invite others to join you or go it alone. Here are some ideas: Put on a play, knit a scarf, choreograph a dance, or conduct a long-term science experiment.

FAST & FUN

You're itching to create, but you don't have much time, and you *might* not have everything you need. No problem! Pick a project you can do quickly with supplies you already have. Draw with colored pencils, write song lyrics, practice a soccer move, or brainstorm ideas for a video game. Or turn the page for more quick creative ideas!

CREATIVITY SPRINTS

Try this just-for-fun activity whenever you need a brain break. Close your eyes and turn the book around two times. Then point to a place on this page. Open your eyes and try the challenge!

Experiment with a new way to shoot a basketball.

Tell the story of your day in a comic strip.

Create an original magazine using cut-up pieces of other magazines.

Think of a new title for your favorite movie.

Make a building out of construction bricks with your eyes closed.

Find a cool object in your house and discover the story behind it.

Make up a dance move.

Draw a floor plan of a new library or the layout of a new skate park in your town.

Doodle an original wallpaper or fabric pattern.

Dream up a new ice cream flavor.

The FUTURE BELONGS to THOSE WHO BELIEVE in the BEAUTY OF THEIR DREAMS.

—Eleanor Roosevelt
Diplomat & Activist

CHAPTER TWO:
IMAGINE

All great inventions, creations, stories, and works of art begin as ideas in someone's imagination. The first step in creating is to dream.

Have you ever wondered where ideas come from? Sometimes they seem to come out of nowhere, like magic. Think about the times you've stared at a blank page or screen, waiting for an idea to arrive (*poof!*) in a cloud of magic fairy dust. Has that ever happened to you?

Maybe it has. (Well, except for the magic fairy dust part.) But most of the time, ideas don't come out of thin air. Ideas usually come from *imagination* working together with *inspiration*.

IMAGINATION + INSPIRATION = IDEAS

Have you ever wanted to write a story but didn't know where to start? Or maybe you have a box of craft supplies and have no clue what to make. If you want to have more creative ideas, you can start by feeding your mind with inspiration.

BIG BAG of INSPIRATION

Inspiration is anything at all that wakes up your imagination. It can be something you

SEE, HEAR, TOUCH, SMELL, TASTE

For example, you might see a cool old photo and start to wonder about the people in the photo, so you write a story about them.

Or inspiration can be an experience or a question. Wondering how rainbows are made might lead you to design a science experiment to discover the answer.

Here are three ways to have more creative inspiration.

● Be a collector.
● Be a detective.
● Be a dreamer.

BE A COLLECTOR

Many artists and inventors—especially those who create on a regular basis—are inspiration collectors. When things come along that capture their attention, they save those things in a special place just like you would a stamp collection or souvenir snow globes. When they hear a song lyric they like, they write it down. If they see a beautiful sunset, they take a photo.

One way to collect inspiration is to write it down.
Here's a page where you can write down some things
you see, hear, touch, smell, or taste that inspire you.

Here are more ways to collect inspiration.

NOTEBOOK

Find an empty notebook. It should be small enough that you can carry it with you. (That way you'll have it whenever you're inspired.) Decorate the cover with paint pens or stickers. Use an elastic sports headband to hold it closed.

BOARD

Start with an empty bulletin board or a large piece of poster board. When you find pictures you like, tape or pin them to the board. Try having different boards for different projects, such as a board for fashion design ideas and another for architecture. You can also ask an adult to help you make an inspiration board on the computer.

BOX

Decorate a cardboard box. Fill it with items that inspire you, such as interesting rocks, seashells, or scraps of fabric or ribbon.

POCKET

Create a pocket in this book! Holding the next two pages together, use colorful washi tape to seal the bottom and side. Leave the top open. Use the pocket to store small, flat things that inspire you, such as magazine clippings or photos. Make more pockets by taping together two pieces of scrap paper on three sides.

BE A DETECTIVE

A second way to get inspiration is to think like a detective. Sometimes questions can jump-start your imagination and lead to creative ideas.

Some of the best questions to ask are **Why?** and **What if?**

Why do leaves change color in the fall?

Why can't people fly?

What if animals could talk?

We'd say we're always hungry!

MY LIST OF QUESTIONS

Try it! Use this space to write your own
Why? and *What if?* questions.

Why _____

Why _____

Why _____

Why _____

Why _____

Why _____

What if _____

What if _____

What if _____

What if _____

What if _____

What if _____

What if _____

QUESTIONS ABOUT ME

Sometimes ideas come from answering questions about ourselves.
Answer the following questions about YOU.

If you could teach any subject, what would it be?
(ANY subject. Even Glitterology or the History of Gummy Bears.)

What activity makes you feel happier than any other?

What's your favorite season? List all the words you can think of to describe it.

If you had to be stuck at the top of a Ferris wheel with someone from history, who would it be?

What's the funniest thing that's ever happened to you?

When you doodle on paper, what do you usually draw?

What's one problem in the world you'd like to solve?

What or who inspires you?

What's your favorite quote?

QUESTIONS ABOUT_____

Think of someone who does a creative activity you would like to do.
(This can be someone you know in real life or someone you don't know.)

Answer the following questions about her or him. If it's someone
you know, ask if you can interview the person. If not, research the
person and answer the questions based on what you discover.

Who are your role models or heroes?

_____

What's your favorite way to be creative?

_____

Do you like to create by yourself or with others?

_____

What's your favorite supply or tool?

_____

What's a form of creativity you haven't tried but would like to?

_____

What or who inspires you?

_____

What is some advice you'd give to people who want to do what you do?

_____

What does your studio/lab/gym/work space look like?

_____

What's your favorite quote?

_____

Who do you ask for feedback?

_____

BE A DREAMER

Sometimes the best way to get ideas is to think or daydream.
This can often be hard because our minds are used to being busy.
Most people don't spend much time staring out the window or at
a blank page. But sometimes our best ideas are just waiting
for our mind to settle down. As you try the activities
in this section, find a peaceful place where
you won't be distracted.

BRAINSTORM

You may have heard about brainstorms at school.

A brainstorm is a way to come up with lots of ideas all at the same time. During a brainstorm, there's no such thing as a bad idea. Just write down whatever pops into your head!

To begin, choose the sort of project you want to do—create a video, write a story, build a robot. Write this at the top of your page. Then write all the ideas (or parts of ideas) you can think of.

VIDEO IDEAS:

fairy tale using action figures

science experiments

paper animation

make a volcano

hairstyle how-to

DIY friendship bracelets

Smoothie recipe

doll stop-motion

interview a grandparent

decorate for Halloween

tour of my city

Keep writing until you run out of ideas—
or there's no more room on the page!

Try it! Write your project on the line below and your ideas in the shapes.

_____

Another brainstorm technique is a called a mind map. To make a mind map, write your creative project in the center of a page inside a circle. Then write any ideas related to the creative project around it. Keep branching off each idea with other related ideas. It might look something like this:

HOW ARE YOU?

Horses that talk

Magical horse

Horses

At a ranch

Action sports camp

Kids at summer camp

Under-water camp

Mermaids

Comic Ideas

Superheroes

Cat superheroes

Detective

MISSING!

Missing pet

Mysterious noises

THUD!

BRAIN BREAK

Sometimes our minds need a chance to play. If your imagination is stuck, try doing something just for fun, such as a word puzzle or number game.

Here's another activity to try. On this page are a bunch of made-up items. Use your imagination to name each one. The sillier, the better!

DESSERT:
Frupie Flip

GADGET:

FLOWER:

CAR:

MUSICAL
INSTRUMENT:
_____

BUG:
_____

ARTICLE of
CLOTHING:
_____

BIRD:
_____

HAIRCUT:
_____

ANIMAL:
_____

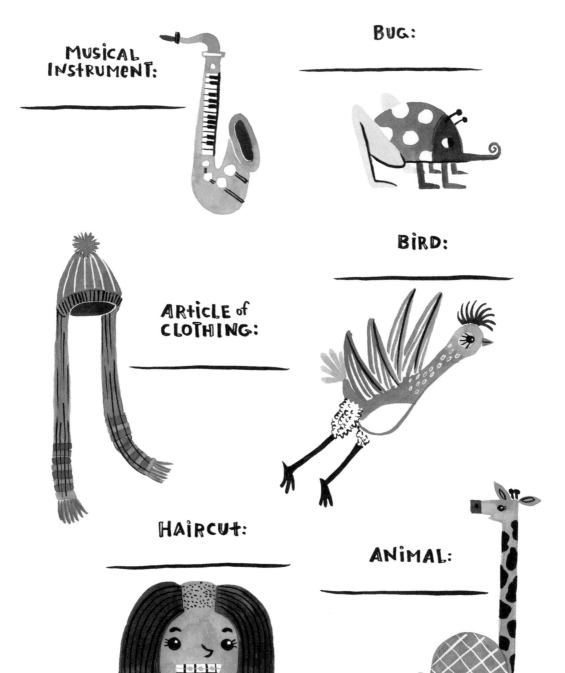

Now it's your turn to doodle. Can you draw each of these made-up items?
(Remember, there are no wrong answers!)

DESSERT:
Blerryblert Cake

ANIMAL:
Long-eared Bizardback

BUG:
Snubble Beetle

GADGET:
Zizzlezip

MUSICAL INSTRUMENT:
Wompet

FLOWER:
Junaflora

ARTICLE of CLOTHING:
Swerf

BIRD:
Swoopdoop

HAIRCUT:
The Panache

CAR:
Radaroo

CREATIVITY TAKES COURAGE.

—Henri Matisse
Artist

CHAPTER THREE:
MAKE

In school you've probably heard of rough drafts. They're the papers you write that no one else sees. But did you know that other things have rough drafts, too? Things like songs, inventions, recipes, crafts—even this book!—all begin as rough drafts.

Another word for a rough draft is PROTOTYPE.

A prototype is the very first version of something. It can be messy and full of mistakes. It's a test, an experiment, a chance to try out an idea.

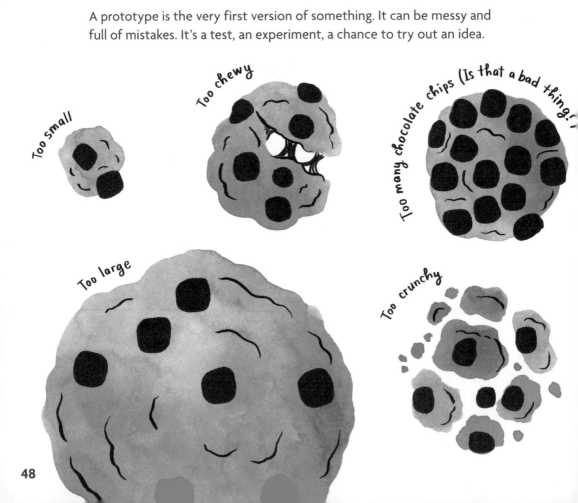

Too small

Too chewy

Too many chocolate chips (Is that a bad thing?)

Too large

Too crunchy

Most things don't turn out on the first try, not even for adults and professionals.

The book you love was probably the writer's third or fourth draft. The photo you find so amazing is the one the photographer took after ten or even a hundred "just okay" photos. The chef who wrote your favorite cookie recipe made a lot of bad cookies first (and probably burned some!).

You don't usually see the burned cookies or the photo where the photographer accidentally put her hand in front of the camera. But that kind of stuff happens to everyone—a lot.

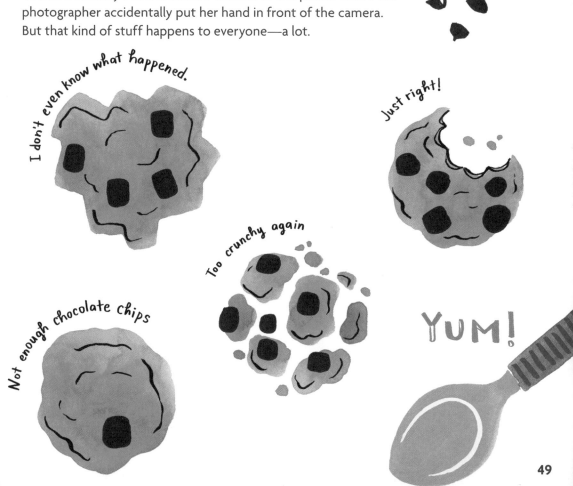

I don't even know what happened.

Just right!

Too crunchy again

Not enough chocolate chips

YUM!

It's normal to get frustrated at this stage of creating. But don't give up!

The truth is, it's easier to start a creative project if you see it as a rough draft instead of a masterpiece that you have to show the world. If you make or do something that doesn't turn out, don't think of it as a failure. Think of it as a *prototype*. Here's a secret about being creative:

YOU LEARN BY MAKING.

And here's another secret:

YOU HAVE TO MAKE A LOT
OF NOT-SO-GREAT STUFF IN
ORDER TO MAKE GREAT STUFF.
PROTOTYPES HELP YOU GET
TO THE GREAT STUFF.

HAPPY ACCIDENTS

Prototypes can also lead to unexpected discoveries.

Did you know that all these items were invented because of a mistake or accident? The next time your creative project doesn't go the way you planned, maybe it'll lead to a different—but still cool—result!

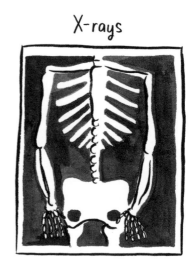

X-rays

Modeling Clay

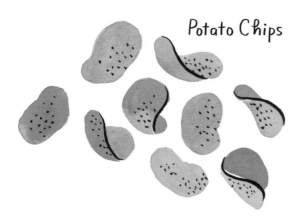

Potato Chips

Matches

Nonstick Coating

Microwave Ovens

Chocolate Chip Cookies

Sticky Notes

Artificial Sweetener

Ice Cream Cones

Paper Towels

53

SUPPLIES & SKILLS

Before you begin a creative project, take stock of the supplies and skills you have and figure out what you still need. It's like packing for a trip. You don't want to get all the way to summer camp and realize you forgot your sleeping bag.

Let's say your project is a

STOP-MOTION ADVENTURE STORY...

Answer the following questions either in your head or on a separate sheet of paper.

What do I have? (supplies, equipment, etc.)
- ☐ a story idea
- ☐ camera
- ☐ action figures
- ☐ animation app
- ☐ toy dinosaurs

What do I need?
- ☐ tripod
- ☐ lighting
- ☐ set

What do I already know how to do?
- ☐ use the animation app

What skills do I need to learn?
- ☐ how to add music and sound to my video
- ☐ how to make a storyboard of my idea

Who can help me?
- ☐ Lucie
- ☐ Ben
- ☐ Dad

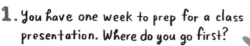

STUDIO SPACE

Where are you most creative? Take this quiz to find out!

1. You have one week to prep for a class presentation. Where do you go first?
   a. The library. The research is your favorite part!
   b. Home. You'd like to practice your presentation with a friend.
   c. A group member's house. You like brainstorming with others.

2. It's a sunny Saturday afternoon. What are you doing?
   a. Trying some new yoga poses outside.
   b. Making a fort for your younger sibling.
   c. Playing softball at the park with your friends.

3. Your perfect pet...
   a. is quiet and cute.
   b. is always ready to play.
   c. follows you everywhere.

4. When you need to unwind, you like to...
   a. play or listen to music.
   b. watch TV with your family.
   c. talk with a friend.

5. Your favorite poster has...
   a. a photo of the ocean.
   b. an inspiring quote.
   c. a scene you can color in.

6. You get to choose your summer camp! Which sounds most fun?
   a. Nature Explorers Camp
   b. Learn-a-Language Camp
   c. Musical Theater Camp

7. Which video are you most likely to watch?
   a. A DIY craft video
   b. A funny cat video
   c. An extreme sports video

8. Which word best describes you?
   a. Laid-back
   b. Talkative
   c. Friendly

9. Your ideal birthday party includes...
   a. a sleepover with your closest friend.
   b. having people sing to you at a restaurant.
   c. a party with your whole class.

Did you choose mostly A's? Then you might like a . . .

SERENE SPACE

When your creative gears are turning, you prefer peace and quiet. Try working in a room that's free from distraction (possibly with a door you can close) and has an uncluttered work space. If that's not possible, wear headphones and listen to peaceful music or background noise such as waves or rain to block out other sounds.

A view of nature

A quiet friend to keep you company

Relaxing music to block out noise

Creativity
takes
Courage

Inspiring quote

Fresh air and
sunshine

S M T W R F S

Plenty of space to
spread out supplies

Did you choose mostly B's? Then you might love a . . .

HAPPY HUB

Even when you're hard at work, you like being in the center of the action. The hum of activity and noise—your dad making dinner or your sister practicing the piano—fades to the background for you and can even energize you. Try working in a common area such as at the kitchen table or on the floor of a family room.

Portable case to store supplies. Try a shower caddy!

People—and pets—to
keep you company

Music and
background noise
to give you energy

A tablecloth to protect
your work surface

61

Did you choose mostly C's? Then you might prefer a . . .

COLLABORATIVE CORNER

It doesn't really matter where you work, as long as there's room for other people to join you! You like team projects where many people work together. Find a place in your house where there's room for everyone to be comfortable. Things can get a little noisy with a larger group, so make sure it's also a place where your volume won't bother others.

Comfy spots where people can sit

Music to motivate you

Space for everyone

THE INNER CRITIC

Once you start a project, sooner or later you'll probably have thoughts like these:

I'll never be as good as so-and-so.

This isn't very good.

Why do I even try?

Maybe the thoughts show up before you even begin. Maybe they wait until you've been creating for a while. Either way, these thoughts are normal.

SAD PATHETIC FRUSTRATED
INSECURE REGRET
DETEST WRONG PANIC
SHAME
UGLY JEALOUS
BORING WORRY
FEAR ENVY
PROBLEM

Remember the journey idea? Discouragement, unfortunately, is a part of the journey of creating something. It's the uphill part, the place where you get rocks in your shoes and start to doubt yourself.

The discouraging thoughts that play in your mind are called "negative self-talk." Some people also call this the "inner critic," because these thoughts sound like a mean voice in your head.

If you listen to these thoughts long enough, they might convince you to quit.

You can try to ignore them, but the most helpful way to deal with them is to:

1. RECOGNIZE THEM.

2. LEARN HOW to RESPOND to THEM.

BACK TALK

If you hear this → then think or say this back. →

"Nothing I do turns out."

" Really? Nothing?
What about that cool
app I coded with Caleb?"

"I can't do this."

"Just because I can't do this
right now doesn't mean it's
impossible. Maybe I need
more practice."

"I'll never be as good
as so-and-so."

"Who says I have to
be like so-and-so?"

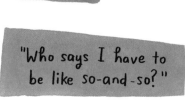

BREAK It UP

If talking back to your discouraging thoughts doesn't work, you might need to take a break.

Do anything that gets your mind on something else for a while. Then go back and add to your idea board, idea box, or idea file.

THE POSITIVITY PAGES

Another way to deal with frustration and discouragement is to think about things that make you happy. After you've filled out this page, turn to it whenever you're feeling discouraged.

Favorite quote

Be you

Do your Best

Draw your favorite place

Favorite color
(color this in)

Another favorite color

Another favorite color

Favorite song playlist

_____

_____

_____

_____

_____

_____

_____

_____

_____

_____

_____

_____

Tape a favorite photo here

I'm good at:

_____

_____

_____

_____

Draw a tiny self—portrait

Draw a tiny family portrait

BE IN THE MOMENT

Still another way to shake off negative thoughts is simply to focus on what you're doing in the moment. Really pay attention and see how many little details you can notice.

If you're drawing at your kitchen table, keep your senses alert as you draw. What sound does the pencil make on the paper? What do you smell? How does the pencil feel as you hold it in your hand? Focusing on these kinds of things can keep your inner critic from getting too loud and free you up to just create.

CAR HORN

MOM'S CHOCOLATE CHIP COOKIES

SCRITCH-SCRITCH-SCRITCH

PAPER IS SMOOTH

INTO A COOL NEW COLOR

ALL SORTS OF THINGS CAN HAPPEN WHEN YOU'RE OPEN TO NEW IDEAS AND PLAYING AROUND WITH THINGS.

—Stephanie Kwolek
Chemist & Inventor

CHAPTER FOUR:
TiNKeR

Once you've made a prototype or rough draft, the next step is to tinker with it or refine it. Think of this as the make-it-better phase. This is when the tweaking, improving, redoing, or fixing happens.

Sometimes the tinkering phase means you create a whole new version of something. You start over, this time using the information you learned from your prototype.

Sometimes it means making some changes to your original idea or adding to it.

And sometimes it means creating the final version of something using more permanent materials.

EVALUA†ION

Before you pull out your paintbrushes again or hit "delete," it's a good idea to evaluate your prototype. When you evaluate, you decide what to keep and what to change. You give yourself feedback. You test out your idea. This feedback can help you figure out what to do next.

Sometimes evaluation is simple. If you code a computer program or design a soccer play, you can test it to see if it works. In situations like these, it's helpful to use something called the scientific method.

When testing something with the scientific method, it doesn't matter how you feel or what you think. What matters is if it works. If it doesn't, you figure out which part to fix. If it does, you're done!

THE SCIENTIFIC METHOD

Ask a question. → Do research. → Write a hypothesis.

Test your hypothesis with an experiment.

Did you get the results you wanted? ←

No

Yes

Troubleshoot the experiment and retest as necessary. Eventually, you may want to use the information you've learned for a new experiment.

Analyze your results. What did you learn or discover?

Your results lead to a new hypothesis and experiment.

Your results match up with your hypothesis.

Your results don't match up with your hypothesis.

Record or share your results.

Like it?

Sometimes evaluation is more complicated. Instead of testing an idea to see whether it works—a simple yes or no—we need to think about the pros and cons. We need to give ourselves feedback.

In today's world, we get and give feedback all the time.

We give a thumbs-up or a thumbs-down.

We click "like," or we don't.

We rate things with stars, hearts, or emojis.

It's easy to look at something and say "I like it" or "I don't like it" and move on. You may react this way to your own creations, too. You think the dance routine you choreographed is good, or you think it's bad.

You like it, or you don't.

End of story, right?

Nope. Whether or not we like something is *one* part of feedback, and it's not even the most important part. The most important part is the ability to explain the *reasons* for our reaction in a way that's meaningful.

In the arts, this is called *critique*. It looks similar to the word *critic* (KRIT-ik) but sounds like this: kri-TEEK.

There are always reasons for our reactions. If we don't take time to think about them, we miss the chance to learn. Reading a story you don't like and being able to describe *why* you don't like it can make you a better writer. Watching a movie and being able to understand why you laugh or get bored can make you a better filmmaker.

CREATIVE CRITIQUE

Try a critique with one of your creations, following the steps shown here. You can write your answers or just think them through.

1. DESCRIBE YOUR CREATION

Stick to the facts, and use your five senses if possible. Don't use words such as "good" or "bad" right now.

-My painting is my house in bright colors.

-The house fills up the whole page. I chose bright neon colors that are not the colors in real life because I wanted it to look like it was from a dream.

-The paint is very thin in some spots, and the canvas shows through.

-There are some places where I dripped paint by accident.

2. See tHE GOOD

What do you like about it? What should stay the same in the next version? Why?

-I love the colors I used, especially the bright pink.

-I like how big the house is.

3. SPOT THE PROBLEMS

What don't you like about it? What do you want to change? Why?

-I don't like the spots where I dripped the paint.

-The top of the roof looks crooked. I want it to be a straight line.

4. THINK OF SOLUTIONS

What are some ways you can address the problems you see? Who can help you look at your creation in a different way?

-Instead of starting over, I want to make changes to this version.

-I'm going to add more paint drips and splatters so that they don't look like mistakes. I think it might add cool texture.

-I'm going to ask my art teacher for tips on how to paint straighter lines and see if I can repaint the edges of the roof.

FRESH FEEDBACK

After you've made your own changes, you might want to get feedback from a friend or family member. Other people can help you look at an idea in a fresh way or lead to new ideas and improvements. When asking for feedback, keep these tips in mind.

1. BE PICKY

When you're testing out an idea or skill, you don't have to show *everyone.* In fact, it's often better if you don't. Instead, ask for feedback from someone who will be honest, respectful, and helpful.

2. ASK GOOD QUESTIONS

It's tempting to ask things such as "Do you like this?" or "Is this good?" But if those are the only questions you ask, you won't get helpful answers.

Here are some examples of questions you can ask about your creative work.

1. What do you like most about my_____?

2. If this was your _____, what would you change?

3. Does this _____ remind you of anything you've seen before?

3. DECIDE WHETHER to USE the FEEDBACK

Just because someone makes a comment or suggestion doesn't mean you have to use it. When it comes to creative work, you're never going to satisfy everyone. There will always be people who like and value what you do, and people who don't. That's okay. You get to choose how to use someone's feedback.

CRITICISM & DISCOURAGEMENT

Here's something you probably already know: Not everyone knows how to give helpful feedback.

At some point, someone will say something about your creations (or about you!) that hurts your feelings. Usually people don't intend to be mean. Sometimes it feels that way, though, regardless of whether it was intentional.

Discouraging criticism is different from helpful feedback. Instead of being respectful and honest and instead of having a purpose, criticism is not useful—and it can be unkind. But remember, just like any other feedback, you can choose what to do with criticism or discouragement. Usually, it's best to let it go and keep on creating anyway.

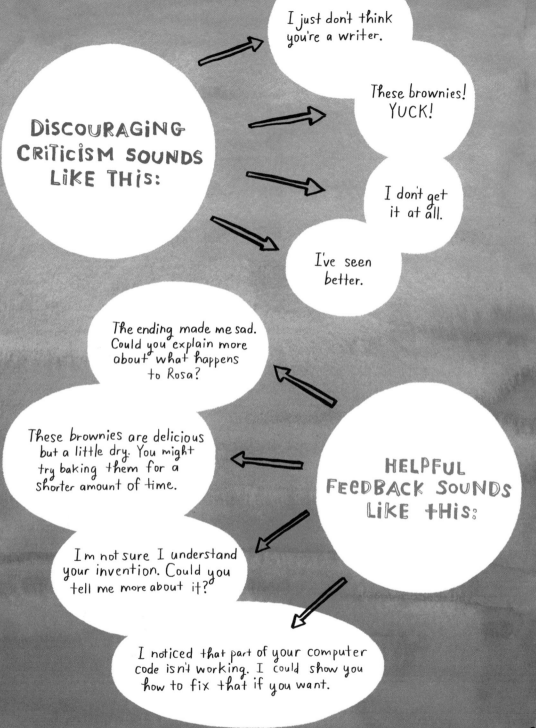

COLLABORATION

Even if you'd rather create alone, there might be times when it's helpful to involve others in your projects. This is called *collaboration*. To collaborate means to work together. Here are some ways to collaborate:

BRAINSTORM IDEAS

DIVIDE UP TASKS

POOL YOUR SKILLS AND RESOURCES

ASK FOR FEEDBACK

Don't know who to collaborate with? Take some time to fill out this list.
Then you'll know who to talk to when the time comes.

Someone who is always full of ideas:

_____

Someone who is good at explaining things:

_____

Someone who shares my hobbies:

_____

Someone who has different hobbies than I do:

_____

Someone who has more experience than I do:

_____

CHAPTER FIVE:
FiNiSH

Eventually all creative projects come to an end. You know you've reached the finish line when at least one of these statements is true:

- ☐ You made all the changes and tweaks you want to make.
- ☐ You're tired of the project or you're bored.
- ☐ Your mind is busy thinking about the next creative idea you want to try.
- ☐ You did what you set out to do. You achieved your original goal.

Notice what this list does *not* say:

YOUR CREATIVE PROJECT iS PERFECT.

It also does not say:

You'RE toTALLY HAPPY WiTH HOW YOUR PROJECT TURNED OUT.

88

When it comes to creativity, there's no such thing as perfection.

And sometimes, as the saying goes:

"DONE IS BETTER THAN PERFECT."

WRAP it UP

Here are some ways to finish a creative project.

SAVE it

Some creations are easier to save than others. If possible, find a special place to store your creation: a box, a drawer, a display area, or a file folder on the computer.

Give it

If you know someone who appreciates your creations, consider giving what you've made to her or him.

To: Grams
♡ Stella

SiGN it

The easiest way to finish an art project is to do what visual artists do: sign your work. In paintings and illustrations, artists often hide their signature somewhere. Sculptors or ceramic artists may sign the bottom of their creations in a place people won't easily see. The work belongs to you whether you sign it or not, but it can help you feel finished. It's like adding a period to the end of a sentence.

NAME it

Give your creation a name or title.

SUNSHINE SONATA

RECORD it

Some creations can't be saved for later, but you can still find a way to remember them: *Take photos or film them.* Keep them for yourself so you can remember what you did. You might even use the photos and videos for future inspiration!

SHARE it

There are many ways to share your creativity with others. Sometimes you can share your creation with the world in a general way: performing a play, sharing a photo or video with friends, or entering a story in a writing contest. Sometimes you can share your creation in a more personal way: displaying it in your room, letting a friend read it, or demonstrating it to a parent.

SCIENCE EXPERIMENT, CRAFT, SPOKEN-WORD POETRY
film it

PLAY, DANCE, SONG
perform it

STORY OR COMIC BOOK
publish it
or
let someone read it

The important thing to remember about sharing your creations is that it's optional. It's okay to create for yourself and not for an audience. Your creative effort still matters, even if no one ever sees it.

You may have heard the phrase *"Dance like no one's watching."* Creating is like that, too. Sometimes it's easier to keep being creative and trying new ideas if you don't have to worry about what other people will think or say. Sometimes you just need to *create like no one's watching.*

THE FiNiSH LiNE is A STARTiNG LiNE

The journey of creating is more like a loop than a one-way road. The ending often leads to a new beginning, and you can make the journey as many times as you want.

So what do you do once the paint's dry, the applause is over, the experiment works, or the video is finished?

You Begin Again

The End

(or maybe... The Beginning)

What sparks your creativity?

Write to us!
Spark Editor
American Girl
8400 Fairway Place
Middleton, WI 53562

Here are some other American Girl books you might like:

Each sold separately. Find more books online at americangirl.com.

Parents, request a FREE catalog at **americangirl.com/catalog**.
Sign up at **americangirl.com/email** to receive the latest news and exclusive offers.

Discover online games, quizzes, activities,
and more at **americangirl.com/play**